Original title:
The Room with a Story

Copyright © 2025 Creative Arts Management OÜ
All rights reserved.

Author: Nathaniel Blackwood
ISBN HARDBACK: 978-1-80587-149-1
ISBN PAPERBACK: 978-1-80587-619-9

Whispers of Forgotten Walls

In corners thick with age and dust,
The walls conspire, as walls often must.
They giggle softly, share a jest,
About the socks, the cat's strange quest.

A tickle fight with breezy drafts,
While sunlight dances, crafting laughs.
The frames of pictures grin with glee,
They hold the tales of you and me.

Echoes of a Timeworn Space

Echoes bounce off creaking chairs,
A bustling party of long-lost fares.
They toast to laughter, spills, and cheer,
While tripping on the playful beer.

The slightly stained old carpet sighs,
With every tale, a secret flies.
It stirs the dust of days gone by,
Where pranks were played and laughter high.

Secrets Beneath the Floorboards

Beneath the planks, a treasure trove,
Of mismatched socks and tales we wove.
The mice chatter in a hushed debate,
About the crumbs and who's got fate.

One springy beam, it bounces back,
Hidden secrets from a snack attack.
Lurking beneath with a giggle and squeak,
The floorboards laugh as we sneak a peek.

Chronicles Enclosed in Four Corners

In every nook, a whisper thrives,
Recording dances of our lives.
The clock on the mantle, it starts to chime,
With jokes of bygone, silly times.

Quirky lampshades share their flair,
Making shadows with a playful air.
They wink and nod, beneath bright light,
Hints of mischief tucked out of sight.

Tapestry of Unwritten Whispers

In the corner, a cat sits still,
Wearing an air of whimsical thrill.
Last week's socks, now a cozy nest,
Who knew they'd turn out to be the best?

The clock on the wall, it never ticks,
But tells tales of time with nifty tricks.
Each tick-tock a giggle, each tock-tick a snort,
It holds more secrets than a jester's court.

Footprints on the Faded Carpet

Strange marks on the floor tell wild tales,
Of pets and mischief that never fails.
A splotch of jam from last Sunday's brunch,
That turned into a sticky, funny punch.

The vacuum once swallowed a sock in its glee,
Now it wheezes and coughs, oh, what a spree!
A dance of dust bunnies twirl in a line,
Who knew a mess could be so divine?

Silent Conversations of Time

The mirror winks at the passersby,
Is it reflecting laughter, or just a sigh?
Each wrinkle a giggle, each frown a jest,
It holds all the stories, simply impressed.

An old chair creaks like a stand-up show,
With each groan, it claims, "I used to glow!"
Chasing ghosts of laughter, on cushions they sprawled,
Silent banter in air, yet never appalled.

The Archive of Forgotten Hopes

Dusty books stacked in a haphazard way,
Hold secrets of dreams that went astray.
One whispers of a knight who was shy,
And another, a dragon who learned to fly.

Each page a giggle, each chapter a punch,
Stories brewed strong, not meant for a lunch.
A library of laughter, where wishes took flight,
In the silence of dreams, joy burns ever bright.

Time's Tapestry of Solitude

In a corner, a sock meets its mate,
Pulled from the depths, can it relate?
Dust bunnies dance in a conga line,
Sharing secrets over forgotten wine.

Clock ticks loudly, a gossiping friend,
Wanting to share, but it won't ever end.
Tangled in tales of days lost in a blur,
Who knew a tick could be such a purr?

A Haven for Heartfelt Confessions

The cat lays low, watching with glee,
As I spill my heart to a cup of tea.
Its nonchalant gaze, a therapist's art,
Purring along as I share my heart.

Grapes on the counter stare down at me,
Whispering softly, 'Aren't we too free?'
In this quirky space where confessions flow,
Even the fridge sighs, 'What a show!'

The Diary of Forgotten Moments

Underneath the bed, old memories lie,
A pizza slice, what a thoughtful goodbye!
Journal entries filled with glittering dreams,
And half-spilled ink, like rainbowed streams.

Dusty old shoes with stories to tell,
Of dance parties where we stumbled and fell.
They giggle each time I pass by in haste,
Recalling my moves, a choreographer's waste.

Whispers Adrift in Stillness

Chairs gossip softly, creaking their views,
On life's little quirks, and our funny blues.
Brooms are in on it, sweeping up tales,
Of nightly adventures, and cake that still fails.

The mirror chuckles at the faces I make,
As I practice my jokes for rehearsal's stake.
In this quiet space where laughter resides,
Even silence can't help but enjoy the rides.

Memories Nestled in the Walls

In a corner, a cat took a nap,
Dreaming of fish in a sunlit trap.
The wallpaper chuckled with each peel,
Whispers of laughter, the sights surreal.

A sock puppet winks from its spot,
Recalling a party that hit the jackpot.
Balloons still float, though the guests have flown,
Each crack a witness, secrets they've known.

Secrets Beneath the Floorboards

Beneath the planks, a mouse plays guitar,
Strumming sweet tunes, a true superstar.
Old boots clatter in a silent dance,
Legends echo, if given a chance.

A dusty old trunk shares its grand tales,
Of pirates, treasure, and wind in the sails.
Yet here it sits, with no one to hear,
Just lost in dreams, covered in cheer.

A Sanctuary of Silenced Tales

On a shelf, a book grins with delight,
While shelves of toys plot a daring flight.
They giggle and scheme, crafting a plan,
To escape the boredom, make a great stand.

A globe spins wildly, lands a bit shy,
Spinning stories of places to fly.
Each map a giggle, each country a laugh,
In this quiet haven, they groove on the half.

Chronicles of Light and Dark

In shadows, a lamp flickers a wink,
Spreading stories faster than one can think.
A paper crane flutters with flair,
Telling old tales while dancing in air.

With laughter that echoes, the clock grins wide,
As time skips along, it's a joyful ride.
So gather 'round, let the nonsense thrive,
In this whimsical space, we feel so alive!

A Diary Inked in Silence

In the corner, a shoe with a tale,
A moth on the wall, donning a veil,
A cat naps loudly, dreaming of cheese,
While a goldfish plots world domination with ease.

An old clock chuckles, hands spinning around,
Tickling the air with its nonsensical sound,
A chair with a story, creaks with delight,
As shadows dance wildly, into the night.

Where Time Pauses to Listen

A rogue sock escapes its dusty abyss,
With stories of laundry, it can't quite dismiss,
A pizza box whispers, 'I'm still warm inside,'
While a note from the fridge seeks a friend to reside.

The table's a witness, with scraps of old cheer,
A mug's wide grin holds the essence of beer,
Dust bunnies giggle, they roll by like kings,
Holding court with the echoes of twenty laugh rings.

Remnants of Laughter in the Air

Balloon animals linger, long past their flight,
Jokes on the walls, like confetti of light,
A rubber chicken, frozen mid-caw,
Awaits on the shelf, a comedic flaw.

A banana peel quietly slips through the years,
Giggling softly, it conjures up cheers,
As the dust settles low, their grins stay alive,
With whispers of laughter where memories thrive.

Threads Woven with Remembrance

Old photos nod with a wink and a grin,
While a hat on the rack dreams of where it's been,
A buckled belt recalls the days it endured,
As hiccups of laughter are gently secured.

A spoon's shiny smile hides secrets untold,
Where soup had a party, both wild and bold,
And jellybeans rally, their colors parade,
In a symphonic clash where the memories fade.

A Space to Breathe Old Stories

Within these walls, odd tales unfold,
A sock that danced, a tale retold.
A cat once wore a shiny crown,
And paraded proudly through the town.

A chair with wheels, it rolled away,
Chasing a dream on a sunny day.
Plants debating, 'Who grows the best?'
While dust bunnies laugh at their jest.

On every shelf, silly knick-knacks,
The rubber chicken makes us relax.
Each corner whispers, "What else could be?"
As laughter peeks 'round, wild and free.

Where Echoes Find Their Home

Here echoes giggle, dodge and weave,
The walls giggle back, they've got tricks up their sleeve.
A broom once swept a surprise so grand,
It's now the star in a dust-dance band!

Tucked in the corner, a hat with flair,
Claims it's the mayor of this wild fair.
Footprints of mischief, a joke on the floor,
Each step brings a chuckle, and who could want more?

A pantry door creaks, its secrets untold,
Whispers of cookie dough stories, bold.
Where laughter resides, and the snickers ignite,
A room full of joy, oh, what a sight!

Threads in the Fabric of Memory

Threads weave smiles, in patterns bright,
A patchwork of laughter, pure delight.
The couch holds secrets of snacks long past,
It chewed an old sandwich, had a blast!

A photo hangs askew on the wall,
Of pets in pajamas, a most epic ball.
Buttons and pins, they plot a scheme,
To sew up the fabric of a funny dream.

Each blanket tells tales of cuddly nights,
Of pillow fights and playful bites.
A tapestry woven, with giggles so sweet,
Where memories dance and never retreat.

Captured Moments in Stillness

Time stands still, but not for long,
In the space where laughter is strong.
A plant once caught a stray balloon,
Now it blooms with a goofy tune!

An old clock chimes, but it's out of tune,
Singing a song to the light of the moon.
With each tick-tock, the giggles align,
In a symphony silly, so divine.

A lowly rug spins tales with a grin,
Of dance-offs and spills, oh, where to begin?
Each captured chuckle, a moment in time,
Breathes life into stillness, sweet and sublime.

Clocks that Ticked in Unison

The clocks all ticked, they had a race,
Yet time stood still, a funny place.
One thought it wise to chime at noon,
While others laughed, 'We'll sleep till June!'

A second clock wore a silly hat,
Said, 'I'm the king! Where's my pet cat?'
The others giggled, spun around,
As minutes danced, still time was crowned.

The hour hand swung like a big pendulum,
Ticking on tales of a jolly rum.
With each tick tock, a chuckle grew,
Why can't clocks be funny too?

In harmony they sang a tune,
Of laughter shared beneath the moon.
Despite the ticking, life was a jest,
In the kingdom of clocks, we laughed the best.

Dusty Tomes of Unlived Life

On a shelf, there sat a book,
With tales of travel, all it took.
A dusty tome, it yearned to speak,
But instead, it just felt bleak.

It dreamed of journeys full of cheer,
Of wacky friends and cold root beer.
But here it sat, its pages crumpled,
In a world where few thoughts fumbled.

The author sipped tea, unaware,
Of all the chaos waiting there.
Each page turned, a zany fun,
Yet dust and time had just begun.

One day, it sighed, 'Let's hit the road!'
With laughs and tales that had been bestowed.
Perhaps a life lived in laughter bright,
Will finally free me into the light.

The Echo Chamber of Yesterdays

In a chamber where echoes play,
The past just loves to have its say.
'Hey, remember when you tripped and fell?'
'Oh hush!' we shout, 'Please, not that tale!'

Each wall reflects a silly prank,
Of childhood dreams and crayons rank.
The laughter bounces, fills the air,
As we embrace the joy laid bare.

A voice from yesteryear pops in,
'You thought you could dance? Oh, what a spin!'
We chuckle as memories swirl around,
In this echo chamber, fun is found.

Yet now, dear friends, let's make new lore,
We'll laugh again right out the door.
Each story told, both old and new,
In this chamber, the laughter grew.

Dances of Light and Memory

In a corner, sunlight plays,
And shadows jump in merry ways.
They twirl and jiggle, dodge each beam,
Creating scenes that make us dream.

Old photos dance like laughable ghosts,
Telling tales of forgotten boasts.
One wore a hat, so tall, so bright,
Said, 'I was best at every fight!'

With every flicker of light's embrace,
Memories pirouette, full of grace.
And in this silly waltz, we find,
A joyful spark, a love unconfined.

So let's join in, don't be shy,
With giggles soft, we'll reach the sky.
In dances of light and tales spun true,
We create a world where laughs renew.

Traces of Yesterday's Dreams

In corners piled with memories bright,
Dust bunnies dance, oh what a sight!
Old socks giggle, tales they weave,
Of lost keys and tricks up their sleeve.

A lamp flickers softly, trying to laugh,
At the cat who sneezes—what a gaffe!
Chairs squeak secrets, they chuckle low,
While the clock ticks by with a lazy flow.

Glimmers of Life Under Dust

Beneath the layers, laughter remains,
A ghostly shuffle in forgotten lanes.
Pictures on walls, they wink and tease,
Caught in a moment, a hint of the breeze.

The old rug grins with stains of a feast,
A comical story of laughter released.
Underneath tables, the crumbs still play,
Whispering jokes from an old buffet.

Murmurs of Home in Every Wall

Walls lean in close, a tale to unfold,
With creaks and moans, they're bravely bold.
A tap of a foot, a snicker from beams,
Carrying echoes of outrageous dreams.

The fridge hums softly, humor in its song,
A joke about leftovers that just feels wrong.
Windows giggle with the raindrops' race,
Each drop a punchline, lost in the chase.

Reflections Caught in Stagnant Air

In stillness linger, a funny old charm,
As mirrors grin wide, causing some harm.
They mimic the frowns of those passing near,
With a wink and a nod, they spread cheer.

The clock's hands freeze, playing a trick,
Saying, "Still here? Better move quick!"
Cobwebs spin tales of laughter and strife,
In this whimsical corner, full of life.

Reflections Captured in Paint

On the canvas, faces grin wide,
Colors splashed, no need to hide.
A jester dances, a dog in a hat,
Each stroke a giggle, imagine that!

Lost in laughter, splattered with glee,
Paintbrush whispers secrets, just for me.
A ceiling that echoes a painter's delight,
Every flick of the wrist turns wrong into right.

From frame to frame, silly tales unfold,
Where winks are exchanged, and giggles are gold.
A landscape of chuckles, a portrait of cheer,
In this painted world, joy's always near.

With every bold color, a chuckle ensues,
In strokes and in hues, we dance, we choose.
So step into laughter, let colors ignite,
In this gallery of humor, everything's bright.

Inhabited by Echoes

Whispers of laughter bounce off the walls,
Tickles of joy in the echoing halls.
Chairs creak with giggles, floors shake with glee,
A symphony of chuckles, just wait and see!

Footsteps of friends, where mischief is born,
Every prank's a giggle, like a child at dawn.
The walls hold the secrets of playful delight,
As echoes of laughter stir hearts up at night.

Silly tales shared, they echo so fine,
Here's to the moments, a bottle of wine.
And though time may pass, these sounds are our friends,
In a place where the laughter never quite ends.

So next time you wander, and hear a light sound,
Know it's the chuckles that dance all around.
This space is alive, with raucous good cheer,
Inhabited by echoes that draw you near.

The Chamber of Unwritten Pages

With pages unturned, destiny awaits,
A pen in hand, it's time to create.
Stories of pineapples wearing bow ties,
Or squirrel detectives catching butterflies!

Ink spills with whimsy, each line a delight,
A cat in a top hat steals giggles by night.
The blank sheets are ready, their stories unknown,
Yet beneath every blankness, hilarity's grown.

Adventure awaits with the tickle of quill,
As squirrels plot mischief, the air's full of thrill.
With tales yet to tell, there's laughter in ink,
In this writer's haven, imagine and think!

So scribble and scrawl, bring laughter to life,
With comedy hiding where silliness thrives.
Each page is a promise of giggles in store,
In this chamber of stories, there's always more.

Silent Witness to Joy and Pain

Silent witness sits, through laughter and tears,
Holding the tales of our hopes and our fears.
A chair in the corner collects the sly smirks,
As it hears all the gossip and all the quirks.

Joy spills like coffee on a Sunday, so bright,
While confessions and giggles drift into the night.
With cushions that know every secret we share,
This place gathers humor with love in the air.

When hearts are so heavy, the couch lends a hand,
With comfort it offers, like humor unplanned.
Through tears and through chuckles, it holds tight the grace,
A silent witness to every wild space.

So next time you linger, recall what remains,
In laughter and sorrow, both joys and the pains.
For this gathering spot, where memories blend,
Keeps silence in check while we giggle and mend.

A Voyage Through Forgotten Stories

In corners where dust bunnies dance,
I found tales that missed their chance.
Each object holds a laugh or two,
Eager to share their view.

An old hat, a shoe, a spoon,
All packed with secrets like a balloon.
With every creak and playful squeak,
They beckon me to hear them speak.

A sailor's map with missing seas,
Whispers of laughter in the breeze.
The couch once held a royal ball,
Now hosts the cat, who thinks it's all.

I'll pour a cup of memory brew,
On each shelf, more than a few.
Let's sail through the giggles and grins,
In this ship where the fun begins.

Rooms that Hold Our Heartbeats

There's a laughter echo in the hall,
A sock puppet ready for a brawl.
Bouncing off the walls with glee,
A secret guardian, just wait and see.

Behind the door where echoes clash,
The tickle monster makes a splash.
Each heartbeat dances in the air,
Shuffling memories, a quirky fair.

The chairs relay their giggles bright,
Tales of chases in the night.
A dance-off held on rainy days,
In this quirky, cozy maze.

With bubbling pots and silly hats,
Every visit, laughter chats.
For every heartbeat that we share,
Is a tickle scare beyond compare.

Echoing Grains of Time

Tick-tock goes the quirky clock,
Where every moment has a shock.
A pile of books stacked oh so high,
They whisper jokes as they fly by.

Here rests the past with a cheeky grin,
Dodging memories like a game of kin.
A bed that once was a launchpad,
For dreams that waved goodbye, how sad!

The floor creaks tales like a comedian,
Imitating a hippo in a medallion.
Each corner bursts with giggles galore,
As if they're all saying, "Let's have more!"

Echoes ripple through the night,
In a stand-up show, a pure delight.
Join in laughter, come take a seat,
In this world where fun can't be beat.

The Shelf of Shattered Futures

Plates stacked high like dreams in flight,
Snapping photos, oh what a sight!
A shelf of hopes, some cracked, some bright,
Each shard a laugh, a spark of light.

Old postcards sent from silly lands,
With doodles drawn by clumsy hands.
The trophies tell of battles won,
While mismatched socks play hide and run.

A jigsaw puzzle missing a piece,
Waiting for a match to find their lease.
With humor lurking in every gap,
Potential poking like a silly slap.

If only dreams could take a bow,
They'd juggle moments, here and now.
On this shelf, laughter's employed,
In shattered futures, joy's enjoyed.

The Guardian of Unspoken Dreams

In the corner, an old chair waits,
For tales of socks and missing plates.
Guarding secrets from yesteryears,
While dust bunnies dance and cheer.

A cactus hides in the sun's embrace,
Winking at shadows that hide their face.
It dreams of travels, oh what a trip,
But it's stuck here – no chance to slip.

The clock ticks loudly, what a fuss,
It measures time in awkward hush.
Tick-tock, tick-tock, here comes the cat,
Knocking down dreams with a swift pat.

So here's to laughter in silent sprees,
Of forgotten dreams, and oddities.
In this place where stories weave,
Guardian smiles, and we believe.

The Other Side of Silence

Beneath the rug, a fortune hides,
Lost marbles and mismatched slides.
A silent giggle from the void,
What a mess the kids enjoyed!

The pictures yell but no one hears,
Captured moments, laughter cheers.
Each frame a tale, a whispered plot,
But most of it? All forgot!

A spider spins a tangled thread,
Crafting stories just overhead.
It chuckles softly, what a weave,
In its world, a grand reprieve.

So in the quiet, let's find the fun,
The giggles never quite outrun.
In the stillness, hear the play,
On the other side, laughter stays.

Whispers of Forgotten Corners

In quiet nooks where shadows creep,
Whispers giggle, secrets leap.
A dust mote twirls, it starts a flight,
Tickling giggles of pure delight.

Old books gossip on the shelf,
Trading tales with dust and self.
Their covers cracked, but oh the glee,
They come alive – just wait and see!

A lonely sock rides on a broom,
Swooping low, it seeks a room.
The lamp chuckles, it knows the score,
Together they dance, spirits soar.

So let us gather, those lost threads,
Of whispered laughter, dreams, and beds.
In corners where the stories blend,
Let's conjure joy without an end.

Echoes in Dusty Shadows

In dusty shadows, whispers play,
Dancing lightly, they sway and stay.
A forgotten hat, it tips with pride,
   Echoing laughter from inside.

A creaky floor, a slamming door,
Jumps and giggles, oh, the roar!
While chairs debate who sits where,
   Echoes linger in the air.

A moth flutters, wearing a grin,
It flits about, where to begin?
Worn-out shoes tap a little beat,
With ragged friends, they shuffle their feet.

So here's to echoes of every kind,
To playful spirits, intertwined.
In shadows cast by fading light,
Laughter lingers, oh what a sight!

The Silence is a Storyteller

In corners old and dusty, tales unwind,
Of socks left behind and laughter entwined.
The echoes of giggles bounce off the walls,
Keeping secrets of mischief that constantly calls.

A chair with a wobble, a table that creaks,
Holds all the whispers of silly critiques.
Timid shadows dance under dim, flick'ry lights,
As time takes a break and the laughter ignites.

The clock on the mantle tick-tocks like a tune,
While the cat on the shelf plots to steal a balloon.
Each creak in the floorboards, a punchline anew,
In this quirky confine where the humor just grew.

A hat on a hook that once belonged to a clown,
Turns frowns upside down, never wears a frown.
In the stillness so funny, stories unfold,
The silence tells jokes and never gets old.

Nestled Within Layers of Time

Beneath the old carpet, the mystery thrives,
Where dust bunnies dance and the wallpaper dives.
A spoon from the '70s, a plate with a grin,
Hiding behind laughter that's woven within.

Once there were parties, all glitter and cheer,
Now just a lizard that grins from ear to ear.
The pendulum swings, whispering tales soft,
Of socks that went missing and hats that were lost.

A thousand brave memories, they gather and play,
Like ghosts at a picnic on a bright summer's day.
A war over crumbs, a crumb that could spark,
The grand feast of ages held dear in the dark.

The clock seems to giggle, tick-tock with a jest,
As time wraps around, giving laughter its quest.
Sealed laughter and folly in layers reside,
In a treasure chest echoing joy deep inside.

Fragments of Joys and Sorrows

In the creases of cushions, laughter is caught,
Like fragments of memories, some bitter, some hot.
A spoon that once stirred up a tale or a stew,
Whispers of joy mixed with wild hullabaloo.

The mug on the table, it's chipped and it's bright,
Recalls the debates on a snowy night.
With stories of triumph, or maybe a fall,
It holds every smile shared within these four walls.

A sock on the ceiling, oh, what a sight!
Yes, it tells of a throw that soared in delight.
The candle that flickers adds warmth to the game,
In tedium's grip, it still plays at the frame.

A picture that's crooked, a grin so absurd,
Yet joy and mishaps are completely conferred.
These fragments sealed tight in a playful embrace,
Bring smiles through the sorrows, time's grand, merry space.

Hushed Voices in the Wallpaper

In patterns a-chatter, the colors collide,
Whispers of laughter wash over with pride.
Each rose holds a riddle, each vine tells a tale,
Of friendly disputes when the jokes would set sail.

The chair's creaky laughter, a small hidden cheer,
A mischief maker that thrives on good beer.
With stories of shenanigans folded like naps,
Unraveled like yarn in hilarious laps.

A calendar hangs with a smile and a wink,
Reminding us all when to giggle and think.
Each day a new chapter of ups and of downs,
As wallpaper chuckles, painting bliss all around.

In silence it hums, in chaos it sings,
Of birthdays and blunders and all silly things.
Hushed voices among blooms, fitting stories align,
In this quirky abode, laughter's simply divine.

Legends Carved into Plaster

In corners where shadows play,
A hero once lost his way.
He tripped over his own two feet,
And now the wall holds his defeat.

Old tales of laughter fill the air,
With goofy grins and wild hair.
A knight in armor—wait, that's a chair!
His epic fail becomes the flair.

Each crack a memory, each dent a laugh,
Of curious souls, a jumbled path.
The echo of pranks upon the ground,
In plastered art, joy can be found.

So gather 'round, let stories unfold,
Of foolish antics and legends bold.
For in this space where giggles blend,
Each wall is a friend that never bends.

The Enigma of Faded Photographs

Snapshots hanging, dust in the air,
Mysterious smiles, a curious stare.
Granny's a spy, we've all agreed,
Next to a cactus, that's quite the lead!

Uncle Bob's pose with his pet iguana,
The dance party moves; oh, what a drama!
A ghost in the image, or just awkward fun?
Every glance at the past brings a giggle run.

Was that a birthday, or was it a prank?
The faces confuse; it's hard to thank.
Time swirls the captions with such little care,
But laughter will linger in every square.

These puzzles we ponder, in laughter we find,
Mysteries of living, comedic and blind.
So cherish these pictures, let the giggles start,
For the heart's little treasures are always the art.

Secrets Whispered in the Dark

The light is low, shadows creep,
Voices chuckle where secrets keep.
A sock lost here, a shoe stuck there,
Whispers of mischief linger in the air.

A cat that talks—or just meowing?
In darkness, the furniture startles and bowing.
Overviewing chaos beneath the cover,
It's hard to find peace when chaos is over.

Giggles and snickers from behind the door,
Power naps interrupted by a snore.
What was that noise? Was that the cat?
The shadows conspire, imagine that!

These tales of laughter float 'round on the breeze,
In corners and nooks, oh, such whimsies please.
So, fear not the night, let laughter ignite,
For secrets in darkness can bring forth delight.

The Lullaby of Aging Corners

Corners creak with a gentle sigh,
Where dust bunnies twirl and time passes by.
An old clock mocks with its silly tick,
Just watch its dance, the moments it picks.

Paint peels like laughter caught in a breeze,
Whispering stories like rustling leaves.
A cane leans close, a buddy so fine,
Together they chuckle, sharing a line.

Memories swing on the cobwebbs' thread,
Of silly mishaps and things left unsaid.
Time flies here, on wings made of cheer,
In mute conversations, life holds dear.

So tiptoe around these corners so grand,
With humor and joy at your command.
For in this haven where giggles abide,
Each aging crevice holds laughter inside.

Ghosts of Laughter and Loss

Whispers of giggles, floating about,
They twirl like shadows, never in doubt.
A tickle of memory, a quirky display,
As echoes of laughter refuse to decay.

When chairs creak softly, it's not just the breeze,
They're sharing old jokes, like a playful tease.
Boots of the past do a silly old dance,
While we caught off guard, can't help but glance.

Each wall has a punchline, each corner a grin,
Ticklish tales linger, they gossip and spin.
Frames hold the past where the gigglers dwell,
In this lively haunt where no one says farewell.

So raise up your glasses to spirits so bright,
They dye the dull air with hues of delight.
For here in the glow of these cracks and squawks,
Together we laugh with the ghosts in our talks.

The Palette of Every Breath

Colors splashed wildly, drips on the floor,
Each hue is a giggle, a banter at the core.
Bright yellows of sunshine, deep blues that cheer,
Every shade tells a tale, so come lend an ear.

A brush with a twist, a canvas of pranks,
Painted with friendship, no need for thanks.
Each stroke is a story, each splash a new laugh,
Creating weird portraits of our quirky path.

Orange bursts forth, like a whimsy parade,
While violets giggle in a bubbly charade.
The palette of breathing, a merry delight,
Where snickers and snorts brighten each night.

So dip in the gaiety, splash on the glee,
These colors come together, just wait and see.
As laughter's the canvas, let's paint it all bright,
With the creatures of whimsy that dance in the light.

Echoed Footsteps of the Past

Pitter-patter echoes, up and down the hall,
Where slippers once sloshed, now shadows just sprawl.
Each scuff on the floor, a tale to unfold,
Of pranks and mischief, and secrets once told.

Oh, the tap of the kettle, and clink of the chair,
Is that laughter I hear? Or ghosts in despair?
A voice from behind says, 'You stepped on my toe!'
While I giggle in silence, is it friend or foe?

Treads of our histories, both silly and grand,
They chase up the stairs, where we once took a stand.
The past can dance lightly, if we give it a chance,
With footsteps that jiggle, and laughter that prance.

Let's follow these echoes, with joy in our stride,
For the party of spirits has nowhere to hide.
In the whims of a hallway, life's dance will endure,
With laughter's soft tap, it forever is pure.

Cracks Like Stories Unraveled

Each crack in the wall is a joke left to tell,
A misshaped old grin, where the odd shadows dwell.
When plaster it wiggles, from laughter or fright,
It whispers the secrets of day and of night.

Tiny splits giggle at the lives that we lead,
How chores turned to capers, and folly's the seed.
Each fissure recalls, how we stumbled and fell,
Into heaps of great fun, and uncertainty's shell.

With stories like puzzle pieces scattered around,
The cracks weave a tapestry, laughter profound.
Let's gather these fragments, put them back right,
With joy from the chaos, we'll dance in delight.

So here's to the mischief, the quirks that we claim,
In this hall of hilarity, we'll brighten the fame.
For every flaw tells us, we're all just a mix,
Crafted artfully, with a few silly tricks.

Timelines Etched in Dust

In a corner, a shoe awaits,
Lost long ago, it contemplates.
A sock claims it was a daring leap,
Now dust bunnies gather, secrets to keep.

Tickling beams from the sun play,
Mice dance, oblivious to the fray.
Yesterday's bill stuck on the wall,
Confessions of snacks, too many to recall.

Forgotten jokes hang in thin air,
Echoes of laughter, stories to share.
A wild cat named Mr. Cheddar stole,
Every last lunch, heart and soul!

With every creak, the house gigs,
Tales of mischief from dancing pigs.
We laugh at the ghosts, their clumsy fun,
In the hallways where daylight wouldn't run.

Windows Wide with Memories

Through panes smeared with life's little bits,
Look closely, and you'll find the wits.
Birds on the ledge, a local troupe,
Chirping their gossip, forming a loop.

Laughter erupts from a cracked vase,
Its floral design now more of a trace.
A squirrel on the sill, plotting a heist,
Nuts in hand, oh! What a feast!

Mud from a flash flood creeps in with style,
Transforming our space, if just for a while.
Memories spill like tea on a worn rug,
Mom's quirky smile from a playful tug.

Each window's a portal to tricks of the past,
A comedy club where shadows are cast.
Fleeting moments in the light's warm glow,
Glimpses of laughter in the ebb and flow.

Murky Waters of Recollection

In puddles of time, thoughts grow hazy,
Reflections of moments, a tad bit crazy.
A fish with a top hat swims by real fast,
Claiming he's the king from the past.

Memory fog, with giggles it churns,
Old tales of pranks that nobody learns.
A hat with feathers, a clown's nose too,
Lurking around, just waiting for you.

In the depths of a drawer, treasures decay,
Keys to nowhere hold whispers at bay.
Marbles and buttons from days gone by,
Unraveling mischief, oh my, oh my!

They dance on the surface and dive without fear,
Playing tag, smelling the skips of the year.
Join in the laughter, take the plunge,
In murky memories, where pasts are unhinged.

The Space Between Seconds

When time holds its breath, moments twirl,
A clock skips a beat, watch it whirl.
In the pause, a humor blooms bright,
As socks have a party, left and right.

The tick-tock laughs, a sneaky embrace,
Sneaking in sarcasm, a playful chase.
Jellybeans tumble from shadows unseen,
A sweetness of chaos where giggles convene.

Mice on the mantel do a little jig,
While the tea kettle sings, a boiling big.
Every second grins, a little unsure,
With laughter as glue, it's hard not to stir.

So cherish the pauses, the wild leaps in air,
In the tiniest spaces, lightness we share.
Embrace every tick, make it count to the core,
For life's just a skit, and we're craving more!

Recollections Adrift in Time

Once I found a shoe, far from its mate,
It had a story, of love and a date.
A sock next to it, with a curious grin,
Plotting adventures with a chipmunk or kin.

There's a dusty old chair that creaks with delight,
Vowing to sail through the stars on a night.
Tales of mischief and grand escapades,
Of how the cat plotted his own charades.

Each photo on the wall has a grin and a tease,
A wizard in shorts and a cat with a sneeze.
As laughter echoes, stories blend in a shuffle,
Discovering treasures, even in the scuffle.

What tales would these objects spin if they could?
Of sandwiches eaten and mysteries understood.
I chuckle and nod, as I ponder and rhyme,
In a corner of chaos, adrift in my time.

The Essence of Enduring Echoes

In the corner, a broom, it dances and sways,
Whispering secrets from long-gone days.
An echo of laughter, a memory's trace,
When a mud pie was tossed, oh, what a disgrace!

A clock on the wall, with hands made of cheese,
Ticking away, breaking all earthly ease.
It chimes every hour with a burp and a squeak,
While mice gather round for a grand game of peak.

Oh, the odd spoon, with a flair so bizarre,
Dreams of stirring soup in a make-believe bar.
With jokes intertwined in each silver shine,
Creating a broth of chuckles divine.

As shadows paint silhouettes, tales intertwine,
The ceiling whispers giggles, sweet and benign.
Embracing the echoes, both wonky and bright,
Each creak makes a memory, bursting with light.

Threads of Memory Intertwined

Stitched memories linger in fabric and thread,
A quilt made of chaos, dreams lightly spread.
Each patch a story, slightly askew,
Of mischievous kittens and a spilt fondue.

A lamp with a grin, it winks from the shelf,
Mocking the shadows that dance by itself.
It giggles in darkness, with a flicker of light,
Casting silly shapes that jump in the night.

Tangled up cobwebs weave tales of delight,
Of misadventures both silly and slight.
They shiver with laughter as dust motes embrace,
Photos of frenzies still stuck in this place.

As the echoes of moments embrace in sweet rhyme,
Threads of a life weave together through time.
In this tapestry vibrant, oh what a sight,
For humor is woven through day and through night.

Within These Walls, A Life Unfolds

Upon these walls, a laughter does ring,
With tales of mishaps, the joy they bring.
A paint splotch resembling a bird in flight,
After a paint fight that spiraled last night.

A table with legs that wobble and sway,
Held up by stories of a game gone astray.
The chairs have conspired, with puns so absurd,
Whispering jokes that only they heard.

Here lies the sock pile, a mismatched delight,
Every woolly character joins in the fight.
The quest for the odd one, a play in this space,
Turns giggles to memories, all set with a grace.

In corners of wonder, adventures will sprawl,
With each tiny mishap that gives birth to a call.
Within these four walls, a life full of cheer,
Where every small moment is cherished, my dear.

Fables Hidden in the Attic

Dusty trunks and squeaky floors,
Bats in corners, opening doors.
A pirate hat, an old boot lost,
A treasure map, at what a cost!

With every creak, the stories laugh,
A puppet show in an empty half.
Ghosts that dance on shelves of cakes,
Silly faces, for goodness' sakes!

A cat in a hat, quite out of place,
Counting coins with a foxy face.
The tales unwound, like yarn on a spree,
Funny fables, come play with me!

A wild giraffe with a dancer's grace,
Twirls with a chair, oh what a chase!
In this attic, joy swirls around,
Where laughter is lost, but always found!

Lantern Light on Faded Pages

In the corner, a lamp flickers bright,
Shadows dance in the soft twilight.
An old book yawns, its secrets spill,
Whispers of antics, laughter, and thrill.

A wizard's wand made of rusted tin,
Turns socks to monsters with a silly grin.
A knight in armor, all dented and bent,
Rides a goose, oh, what a twist was meant!

With every word, the pages tease,
Stories tangled like wrestling bees.
An owl hoots, wearing specs for style,
Reading out loud, it stays for a while!

Lanterns sway with the night's grand song,
Sketching adventures, where laughter belongs.
Old tomes giggle and flutter with glee,
In this funny world, come join the spree!

A Haven for Forgotten Souls

In the attic, shadows know their songs,
Where the forgotten, the fabulous throngs.
A toothless dragon, snorting out smoke,
Tells tales of treasure, oh what a joke!

A ghost in a cape, with a clownish grin,
Plays hide and seek, where do we begin?
Near the window, a jester's hat,
Sipping lemonade, how 'bout that?

Old photographs, faces all askew,
Waltzing and tripping, what else could they do?
Cupid's arrows, now tangled in vines,
Shoot candy hearts and jumpin' designs!

In the whispers of dust, mischief is sought,
Laughter rings out from the stories they brought.
A haven for souls, where nonsense is king,
Silly and splendid, let the laughter ring!

In the Nook of Recollections

Nestled in corners, memories dance,
A polka-dotted bear, takes a chance.
With a pop and a twirl, it sings quite loud,
Stories wetting smiles, like rain on a crowd.

The cupboard creaks with a playful grin,
Hiding trinkets, where mischief begins.
A pair of old shoes, they stomp and shout,
Trying to find what they were about!

Socks that vanished, giggling in shame,
Sneak out at night, just to play their game.
A raccoon in slippers, oh what a sight,
Swings from the rafters, with pure delight!

In this nook, the laughter grows bright,
Whimsy and wonder in the soft moonlight.
A treasure trove full of silly charms,
Come join the fun, and spread open your arms!

Fragments of Lives Once Lived

In a corner, dust bunnies stand,
They argue who made the biggest strand.
A sock puppet grins, with a solitary cheer,
As the chair creaks tales, yet nobody's here.

The mirror cracks jokes, of hairdos gone wrong,
While the clock ticks nostalgia in a curious song.
A shoe from the '80s claims it can dance,
But the couch just rolls its eyes at the chance.

An old book whispers secrets, bound in delight,
Of spaghetti dinners and epic pillow fights.
The cat sneaks a peek, with a glance so sly,
"Oh, what a weird past! How time seems to fly!"

Beneath the wallpaper, the wallpaper peels,
Each layer a memory, each story reveals.
They laugh at the time, with a wink and a nod,
Here's to all life's quirks! Let's give a loud prod!

Echoes of Laughter and Tears

In the chair by the window, laughter is stuck,
It tells tales of mishaps, not one of good luck.
A mug chips in, with tea spills so grand,
"Oh dear," it sighs, "I never had a plan!"

The rug feels the giggles, a ticklish affair,
As dust clouds dance with tricks in the air.
A dog with old bones shakes just to fit,
While the TV rewinds to the time that was lit.

A vase claims it's crafty, it holds up a grin,
"Remember the party that I couldn't begin?"
The plants nod in rhythm, with leaves draped in cheer,
Whispering stories of every guest near.

With shadows as guests and echoes for sound,
This space holds the laughter that knows no bound.
Amidst all the chaos, a feather drifts by,
In moments so silly, let's all just apply!

The Canvas of Quiet Moments

In the nook where all whispers are tender and light,
Paint splatters joy, a colorful fight.
An old shoe grumbles, "I've walked all around,"
While pondering feet that make circles unbound.

An easel looks up, with an arch of its back,
Pondering portraits of the things it could lack.
It sighs with delight of each brushstroke's lore,
"More colors give life, than the dull ever bore!"

There's a pen with a cramp, unable to write,
And a notebook with dreams that say, "Give me flight!"
The surrounding silence holds stories to tell,
Of moments once lived, where laughter once fell.

Hours drip down, like a candle that sways,
Each flicker captures both the laughter and praise.
In quiet reflection where stories collide,
Every corner whispers what time couldn't bide.

Dust Motions in Sunlit Beams

Under sunlight, dust dances like sprites,
Waltzing and twirling in whimsical flights.
A chair sighs its tales from the burdens it bore,
While shadows look on, always wanting more.

The floorboards creak with a laugh and a joke,
As they share all the secrets that morning bespoke.
A forgotten toy swings, still full of delight,
Chasing shadows of laughter, from morning till night.

A duster sits proudly, a feathered knight,
Fighting against grime with all of its might.
"Every sweep tells a tale," it puffs with a grin,
"Of all that has happened, we'll conquer again!"

With warmth in the corners, and stories to save,
Each bit of the dust is a memory's wave.
In beams of bright sunlight, let's dance a bit near,
For laughter entwines with each flicker of cheer.

Where Memories Lace the Curtains

In a corner, a hamster wheel spins,
While socks mysteriously face off again.
Old chairs whisper of ancient debates,
As dust bunnies host their wild estate.

A clock ticks loudly as if it knows,
The time to gossip, the time to pose.
Jars of buttons, each with a tale,
Of fashion trends that are far from pale.

A painting stares, with fruit on display,
Wondering how it's still here today.
The cat naps softly, dreams of fish,
In this cozy chaos, all are delish.

Underneath the floorboards, secrets reside,
Where memories dance and giggles collide.
Each trinket a tale, each crack in the wall,
A legacy whispered, a raucous ball!

Portraits of the Unliving

In the gallery, portraits chat and chime,
With jokes from the past, they share their prime.
A dog with a bow tie shows off his flair,
While Uncle Bob just can't seem to be there.

Each frame a witness to laughter and tears,
With stories of pranks from the yesteryear.
A faint chuckle echoes from one faded face,
While another insists on a timeless grace.

A coat rack speaks, 'I'm more than a guise!'
Collecting the tales of all who have been wise.
Each hat on a peg has a story to tell,
Of days gone by, and the laughs that befell.

The wall's peeling paint quips, "A style so chic!"
With exclamations of when they were at their peak.
In this lively gathering, with memories so bright,
It's a gallery of whimsy, igniting delight!

Shadows that Speak in Color

In the dim light, shadows weave their dance,
Gossiping silently of a fleeting chance.
A curtain flutters, a playful tease,
Tickling the air like a breath of breeze.

The floorboards creak, echoes of old plays,
With mischief lurking in the sunbeam rays.
A silhouette of a cat makes a leap,
While chairs murmur tales that never sleep.

The walls are alive with passwords of fun,
Each crack revealing a secret or pun.
A ghost that was never quite left the scene,
Remains to ensure the party's routine.

Laughter and giggles, colors collide,
In shadows that know where the secrets reside.
This hall of whispers, a canvas alive,
Where memories spark and the spirits thrive!

Timeless Vignettes in Stillness

In the echoing silence, moments rewind,
Where laughter and whimsy are intertwined.
A teapot grins with a knowing glance,
As spoons share tales of a curly dance.

The rug remembers each scamper and slide,
While a clock rolls its eyes at the time it's defied.
Dust motes swirl like confetti in plays,
Celebrating life in curious ways.

Photos glance back like old friends turned wise,
With secrets and smiles that never disguise.
Each frame adorned with quirks and delight,
Preserving the silly through day and night.

Amid stillness, warmth flitters around,
A world where whimsy and stories abound.
These vignettes of life cling to a thrill,
In this cherished haven, time stands still!

Between the Walls

In corners where whispers dwell,
A sock once lost begins to tell.
It giggles loud, a tale so bold,
Of funky days and youth untold.

A spider spins its chatty thread,
Of all the shoes it wishes fed.
It laughs at dust and crumbs that fall,
A kingdom vast, within these walls.

An old chair creaks, it knows too well,
The secrets of the folks who fell.
It grins, recalls a wild old dance,
And shakes its legs to give a chance.

So here we sit, with tales grand,
Among the clutter, hand in hand.
With laughter's echo, stories fly,
Between these walls, they never die.

a Heartbeat

In this cozy nook of time,
A feathered hat begins to rhyme.
It jokes of days the cat had fun,
With mice that danced beneath the sun.

A lamp that flickers, winks with glee,
It knows the secrets, just like me.
It crackles laughter in the night,
With shadows swirling, oh what a sight!

A clock that ticks with a silly beat,
Sings to the shoes that refuse to meet.
'Time's a jest,' it seems to say,
'Let's spin around and play all day!'

So let's laugh loud, and dance for fun,
This heartbeat room 'til day is done.
Each tick a giggle, each tock a cheer,
In this funny place, we hold so dear.

Realms of the Unspoken

Here lie the dreams beneath the bed,
A hat that fits on a crooked head.
They snicker softly, taking flight,
In realms unseen, from day to night.

A blanket fort, the rooftops high,
Where silly giggles float and fly.
The voices of the toys conspire,
To tell the tales of dreams on fire.

The door creaks loud, it wants to play,
Inviting giggles, come what may.
Each corner hides a sneaky laugh,
In realms of joy, we dance and wrassle.

So close your eyes and take a peek,
At realms where fun and laughter speak.
Adventure waits just out of sight,
In silly shadows and pure delight.

Murmurs from the Shelves

On dusty shelves where stories sigh,
A novel nudges, 'Oh, come try!'
It winks at poems stacked so neat,
Crafty tales of love and defeat.

A cookbook giggles, what a delicious scene,
Of pie-filled dreams and raspberry cream.
It whispers sweet, 'Don't judge too quick,
For every recipe hides a trick!'

The globe spins round, a silly show,
'Round the world in a day, let's go!'
With every label, a jest and a laugh,
These murmurs unveil a fun-loving path.

So take a stroll through this bookish land,
With every turn, there's joy at hand.
Let laughter bubble, let stories swell,
In this haven of murmurs, the heart will dwell.

Windows to Lost Dreams

Through panes that sparkle, sunlight beams,
Revealing whispers of lost dreams.
A kite that flew but never came down,
Is tangled in the curtains' crown.

With every breeze, it tells its tale,
Of high-flying hopes that set the sail.
It flutters gently, a ghostly swoon,
Daring daylight, hiding in June.

A forgotten toy peeks through the glass,
Waiting for kids to join the class.
It chuckles low, 'Oh what a game,
To see grown-ups forget their name!'

So lean in close, and breathe it in,
The laughter echoes, let's begin.
These windows wide invite us all,
To gather 'round at the whimsy's call.

Strokes of Time on a Stained Canvas

Splashes of paint with tales to tell,
Each brushstroke whispers, 'I fell!'
A cat in a hat, a dance of socks,
Under the table, a pair of rocks.

A clock with no hands, ticks just for fun,
It laughs at the sun, then hides from the run.
Silly old ghosts in polka-dot shoes,
Stepping on dreams, sharing the blues.

A chair that spins, a wall that can talk,
With echoes of laughter, it starts to mock.
Mismatched curtains in colors so bright,
They giggle at shadows that dance in the night.

And here on this canvas, stories collide,
With capers and mishaps we cannot abide.
As time drips and spills from a goblet so bold,
Life's foolish escapades are a sight to behold.

Memories Clinging to the Ceiling

Sticky notes flutter like butterflies bold,
Each one a secret, a story retold.
Old teddies grinning from high up on shelves,
Whispering jokes to the dust bunnies' elves.

A ceiling fan spins like a whirlpool of cheer,
Chasing lost thoughts that vanish from here.
Paint cracks in laughter, reminding us all,
Of moments so silly, they rise and they fall.

Cobwebs are tapestries woven with glee,
Reminders of times when we climbed the wrong tree.
The lightbulb above flickers, plays peek-a-boo,
Laughing at memories of what we once knew.

A hall of reflections, where chuckles abound,
Imbued with the magic of joy all around.
With each glimmer of laughter stuck up on high,
These memories dance, and they never say goodbye.

Where Dreams Sprawl in Corners

In the nooks and the crannies, dreams play hide-and-seek,
Humming old tunes, oh so uniquely oblique.
A sofa that snores, what a curious fellow,
While pillows conspire, soft and marshmallow.

A fishbowl holds secrets, and bubbles of glee,
Tales of the deep swimming wild and free.
Chairs tell their stories in creaks and in groans,
As socks find companionship with lonely old phones.

Popcorn kernels jump, hiding just out of sight,
Tickling the cat, oh what a delight!
Under the rug, a lost shoe starts to scheme,
Plotting to join in on the next silly dream.

Walls that might giggle, all jagged and thin,
At the jokes of the past that tumble and spin.
In corners where laughter and whimsy collide,
The magic of dreams flows, like a fun-loving tide.

A Chamber of Wants and Wishes

A treasure chest bursting with mismatched delight,
Filled with old hopes and dreams taking flight.
A clock made of candy, tick-tock with a lollipop,
Each second a giggle, sweet sugar we drop.

Postcards from places where rubber ducks roam,
All penned by the wishes that call this place home.
A wishing well filled with socks on the loose,
Each toss brings a chuckle, as time starts to juice.

Balloons with a message float high toward the sun,
They whisper, 'We've all had our share of the fun!'
And a pair of old shoes with tales from the past,
Join in with the laughter, they'll make memories last.

So here in this chamber, where wants intertwine,
Laughter and wishes tiptoe the line.
With hopes that are silly and smiles that are wide,
This place is a playground where joy can reside.

Murmurs from Within the Hearth

In the corner, shadows cheer,
Old socks dance, oh so near.
The cat's debate with a spoon,
Tickles the light of the moon.

Crumbs scatter, tales arise,
From the floor, to my surprise.
A rogue potato sings a tune,
Jokes echo from the old maroon.

Echoes of giggles float and sway,
Mice in hats both laugh and play.
A kettle whistles jokes so bright,
Steaming up in sheer delight.

Portraits of Long-Lost Laughter

Framed in dust, the smiles freeze,
A rabbit potting plants with ease.
Grandma's cookies, a friendly tease,
Whiskers twitch, as laughter flees.

Pirate spoons joke on the shelf,
Each speaks tales of a digit elf.
Whispers of chaos in the air,
As colored socks engage in flair.

Ticklish curtains swish about,
Chasing dreams made of chocolate stout.
Secret parties in the night,
With zebras playing cards—what a sight!

The Memory-Maker's Oasis

Under a blanket, laughter hides,
With lost sock puzzles and wild rides.
Teapots giggle at daily news,
While spoons conspire with old shoes.

Wobbling chairs tell silly tales,
Of snorting cats and giggling snails.
Pillow fights with thoughts of delight,
As evening settles, laughter ignites.

Mirthful echoes from old walls,
With whimsy that endlessly calls.
Each creak a whisper of well-kept fun,
Crafting memories—never done.

Stories Woven in Dust

In the corners where secrets sleep,
Toys renegotiate the leap.
Dust bunnies host a grand parade,
While old vacuums joke, unafraid.

Silly hats on mannequin heads,
Dancing shoes among the beds.
Each trinket has a tale to share,
Of sock wars and wild summer flair.

Giggly ghosts roam the halls at night,
Turned portraits swirl in soft moonlight.
With every creak, a chuckle can bloom,
In a never-ending, whimsical room.

Knots of Emotion Tied in Space

In a corner, a sock lays lost,
Each wrinkle, a tale of the cost.
The cat finds it, a prize in her eyes,
While the owner just sighs with surprise.

A spaghetti noodle dances near,
It sways like it has no fear.
With thoughts of marinara sauce,
It dreams of a feast that's worth the gloss.

The clock ticks with an awkward beat,
Chasing its hands on mismatched feet.
Ticklish laughter echoes around,
As secrets in the air are found.

Puzzles with missing pieces reside,
Questioning life's great, silly ride.
Each odd piece fits in a way,
Only in dreams do we play.

Pages Turned on Invisible Hands

Books stacked high, a tower of tales,
Windy whispers and crazy gales.
A chapter read, then flipped around,
As if by magic, the plot unwound.

Each dog-eared page has something to share,
Spilling secrets and mishaps rare.
An author chuckles at the twist,
While readers ponder what they missed.

The ink sometimes giggles, it appears,
As if spilling all its hidden fears.
A plot that thickens, then lightens the mood,
Winding in circles, a literary feud.

So many sentences, sentences so funny,
Each line worth more than a bag full of honey.
With a turn of a page and a wink of an eye,
The world of words begins to fly!

Starlit Shadows at Dusk

Under the moon's quirky glow,
A shadow winks, all aglow.
With starlight giggles, it leaps about,
Pretending to dance, oh what a clout!

Crickets hum a ticking tune,
While frogs in tuxedos croak and swoon.
A night like this, pure, silly delight,
As laughter echoes into the night.

Jars of fireflies blink like stars,
Joining in laughter from afar.
Each little glow has a line to say,
As if they've all come out to play.

The breeze tells jokes from the trees,
While daisies grin with such ease.
In this twilight, where shadows recede,
Silly moments plant a heartfelt seed.

Tales Woven in Worn Out Rugs

Beneath our feet, stories unfold,
In threads of laughter, bright and bold.
Each stain a sign of joy and regret,
A dance on the floor we won't forget.

Shapes that wiggle and jiggle in place,
As if each fiber's found its space.
A cat leaps high, claiming her throne,
While the dog curls up with a joyful groan.

The tassels sway like silly sprites,
Winking as they share their delights.
With each step, secrets are shared,
As life on this fabric is hilariously bared.

So many moments tucked tight and snug,
In the colorful fibers of this old rug.
When the sun dances, the stories spin,
Laughter's the prize, where tales begin!

www.ingramcontent.com/pod-product-compliance
Lightning Source LLC
Chambersburg PA
CBHW060123230426
43661CB00003B/308